ADVANCED EXPLOSIVE KICKS

ADVANCED EXPLOSIVE KICKS

by Chong Lee

AUTHOR OF
DYNAMIC KICKS

Printed in the United States of America
Library of Congress Catalog Card Number: 78-61152
ISBN No. 0-89750-060-1

Sixth Printing 1980

OHARA PUBLICATIONS, INCORPORATED
BURBANK, CALIFORNIA

DEDICATION

I would like to dedicate this book to my younger brother, Chong Bum Lee, of whom I am very proud.

ACKNOWLEDGEMENT

John Vaneck, a most dedicated student who appears in these photographs, has also been a good friend and source of personal inspiration, for which I would like to thank him.

For all her typing and help with the language, Patty deserves and is granted more gratitude than can properly be expressed here.

ABOUT THE AUTHOR

A quick flipping-through of the following pages should suffice to convince that Chong Lee is a man who can kick—kick with power, speed and accuracy. But these kicks, as you will find if you take this book off somewhere to try your legs at a few, do not come exactly easily. Moreover, unless you're already something of an expert, it will probably take you years to snap off kicks with the pile-driving force Chong Lee unleashes.

For although he's still young, Chong Lee has had many years already to perfect the fighting style that helped him win the Forms Grand Nationals in Long Beach in 1974. Leaving child's play to other children, Chong Lee took up *ji do kwon* at age five. Under the watchful eyes of Chong Byung Wha, the boy trained religiously. Thus, it is not hard to believe that by age seven, wearing his newly acquired black belt, he was much in demand at demonstrations and exhibitions.

At 11 he enrolled in an academy of Thai boxing which was, literally, a school of hard knocks. Here he broke his forearm, numerous toes, and had his jaw fractured on two different occasions. Nonetheless, he persisted for two years, learning to take blows as well as deliver them.

Later, having immigrated with his family to America, Chong Lee was introduced to American noncontact karate. But having so many years of full contact under his belt, it took him years to make the necessary adjustments in his fighting style. He was continually disqualified during those days for landing kicks and punches. Worse, he sometimes lost bouts he might have won by exhausting the best of his concentration in trying to suppress and restrain his attacks. Though he finally learned to adapt his kicks, he is now mostly involved in forms and free contact—a rare combination, perhaps, but one that suits Chong Lee.

In 1975, having decided to teach *tae kwon do*, Chong Lee established a karate studio in Tarzana and discovered that some of his students would travel as far as 50 miles several times a week to put themselves under his instruction—this in a city like Los Angeles where there are dojo in almost every neighborhood. From four until nine, five nights a week, Chong Lee instructs, as he says, "strict and thorough." That he is an able, even gifted instructor has been established by the successes of his students in tournaments throughout the world.

Sleep till noon? No, not Chong Lee. His daily schedule keeps him about as busy if not as exhausted as a typical Marine recruit in boot camp. "When I first came to this country," he says, "it was all karate, all punching and kicking. I couldn't speak English very well, so I had to be a good kicker. But then I began to sense opportunities all around me, and I began to feel like a machine."

Feeling as though he didn't necessarily want to spend the next 50 years of his life kicking and punching, Chong Lee enrolled in pre-law at the University of Southern California in Los Angeles. Scheduled to take his degree in June of '78, he hopes to continue in school and earn his Master's in Business Administration the following year.

School has made a big difference in his outlook. "Before, my life was karate—one hundred percent," he recalls. "Now I'm more open; I have more respect for individuals both in and out of the martial arts. Still, when I'm teaching I'm very strict. But after class I relax. During class it's 'do this, do that.' After class it's 'Good night, Mr. Smith.' "

Up at six and to bed at midnight. Yet with all this, Chong Lee has other pursuits and interests, particularly running and flying. He hopes to begin lessons and earn a pilot's license sometime in the not-too-distant future, and perhaps we ought not think his interest in flying all that unusual. Take a look at these kicks. Though he doesn't have wings, Chong Lee has spent, as we can see from the photographs, a lot of time in the air already.

PREFACE

Of all the techniques used in the martial arts, perhaps the most difficult to master are the kicking skills. Successful kicking employs, often under great stress, muscles that are little used in ordinary daily activities. Beginners, especially, are cautioned to beware of the straining and tearing that can result without proper limbering and stretching exercises. In executing many of these kicks, even an otherwise relatively accomplished martial artist can expect difficulty and frustration unless he takes time to warm up.

On the other hand, there are basic physical laws or principles based on certain anatomical similarities, and these common resemblances govern the movements of all would-be kickers. This book concerns itself with instructing the reader in how to make more efficient and powerful use of his legs.

Chong Lee, known as one of the country's top kicking specialists, here presents an ideal opportunity to study virtually perfect kicking form. But the reader is asked to bear in mind that all the kicks illustrated here are photographed in their most extreme forms. The reasoning? Although kicks are not always thrown high or at the head, it is further from the feet than any other likely target. If a martial artist can deliver controlled strikes to an opponent's head, landing those same blows on lower, more accessible targets will be that much easier. Simply put, proficient kicking enables the fighter to deliver explosive power to targets that cannot be reached with the hands.

Though somewhat more advanced than the kicks offered in his earlier book, *Dynamic Kicks*, these movements are basically accessible to the person of average physical endowment—provided only that the reader will take the time to develop himself. Variations can make these kicks more practical for students of differing builds, even if the variations diminish, slightly, the total power that can be delivered in these kicks. Experiment.

Explosive Kicks and Applications is a response to the widespread acclaim and enthusiasm of student and instructor alike for *Dynamic Kicks*, and as a slightly more advanced book, was written to expand on and supplement concepts and kicks set forth in the earlier work.

CONTENTS

Kicking 12
Stretching Exercises 24
Single Kicks 44
Complex Kicks 86
Sitting Kicks 118
Take Downs 128

KICKING

STRIKING AREAS

As far as kicking is concerned, the martial artist may choose to kick with any of nine different surfaces. Blows delivered with the heel are intended to land either on the bottom or back of the heel. In either case, curl your toes and instep up toward your knee. To strike with the ball of the foot, point with your instep while pulling back with your toes. To hit with the arch of the foot (the area between the heel and ball), you may either point your foot slightly as you would do in executing sweeps, for example, or the foot may be angled in toward the knee as in side kicks and stomps. Kicks thrown with the outside edge of the foot are executed with the arch curved inward toward your knee in order to insure that the outside area of the foot makes primary contact.

HEEL

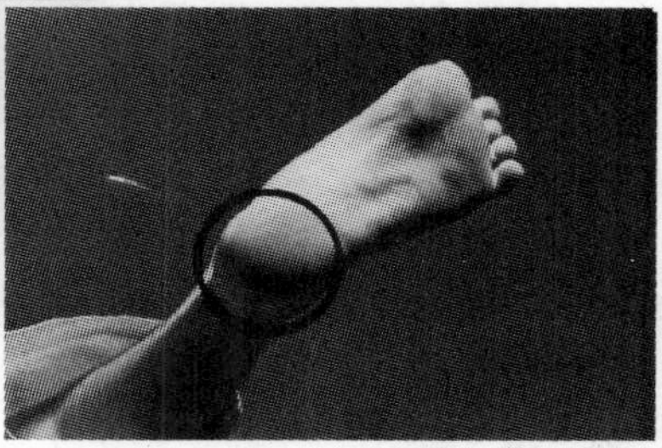

BALL OF THE FOOT

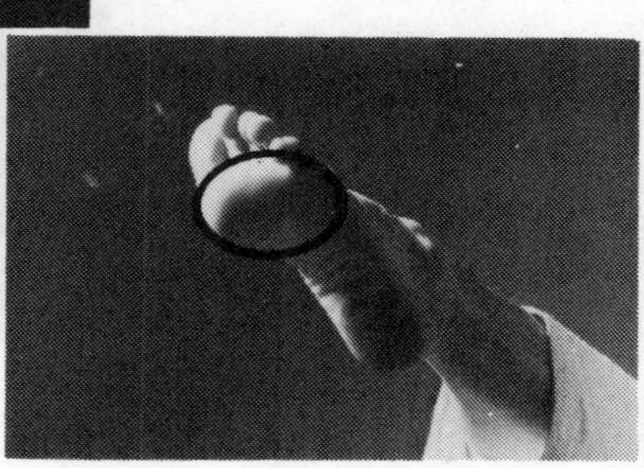

INSIDE OF THE ARCH

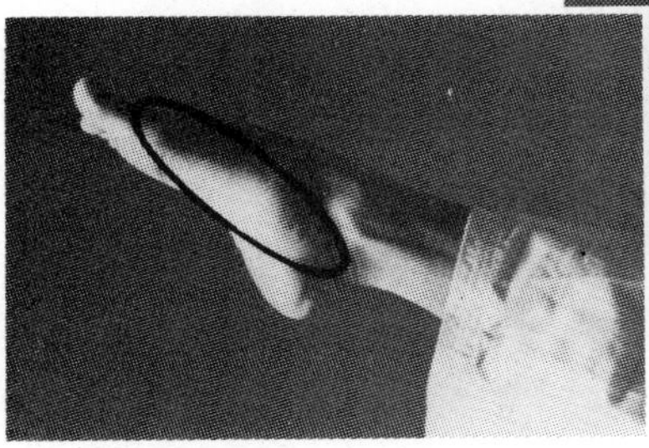

(FOR INSIDE CRESCENT KICK)

OUTSIDE
CRESCENT-SHAPED AREA

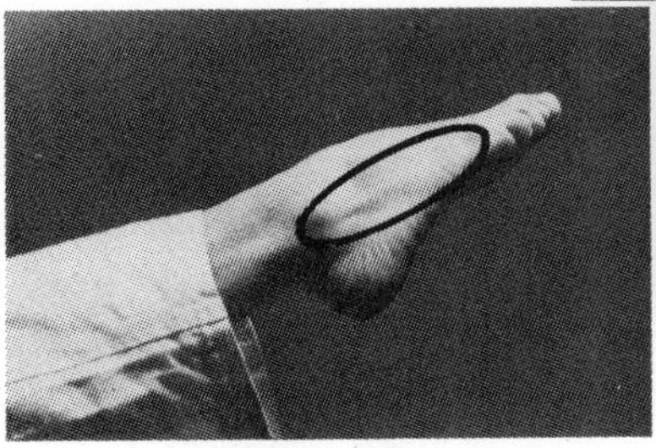

TOP OF THE INSTEP

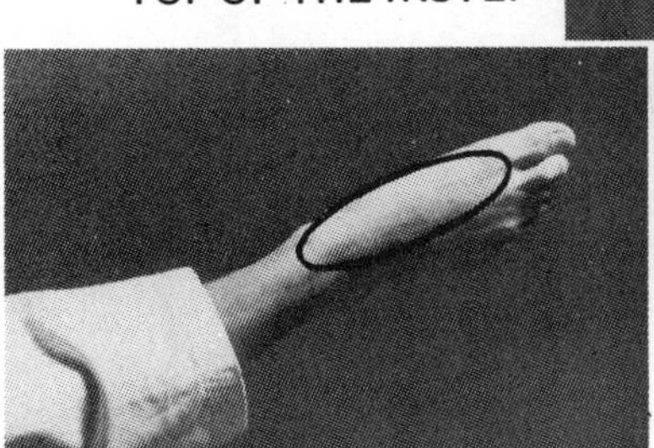

(CONTINUED)

(CONTINUED)

EXTREME OUTSIDE EDGE OF THE FOOT

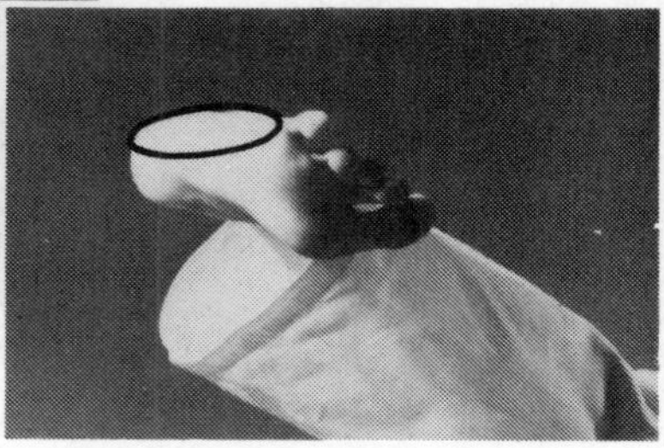

KNEE

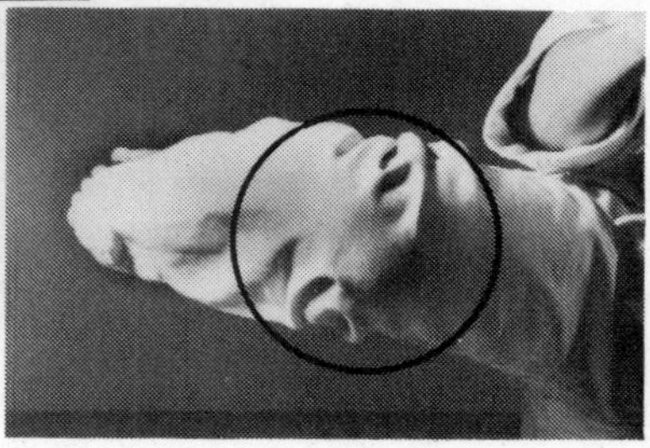

BOTTOM OF THE FOOT

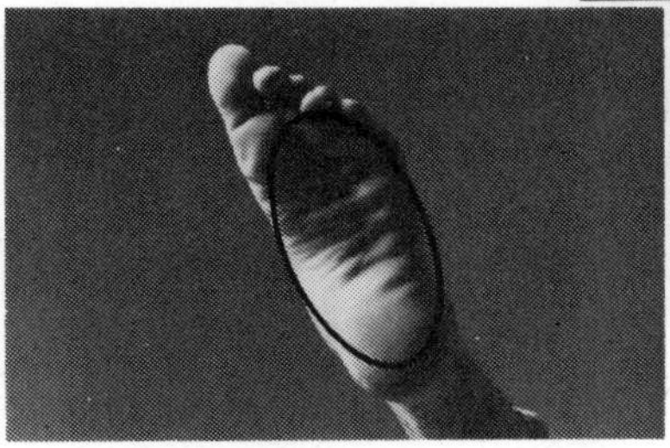

SHIN

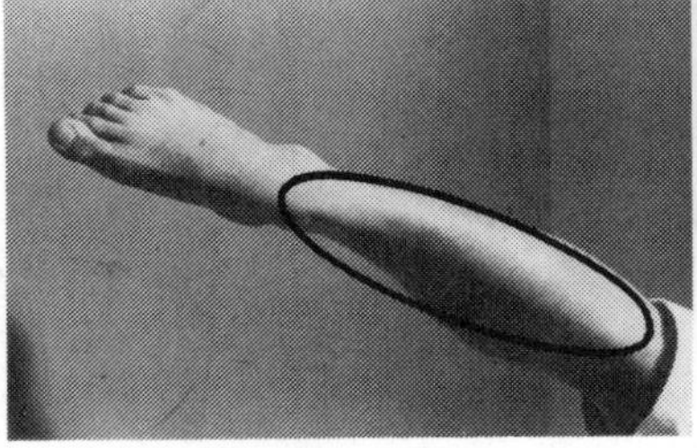

TARGET AREAS

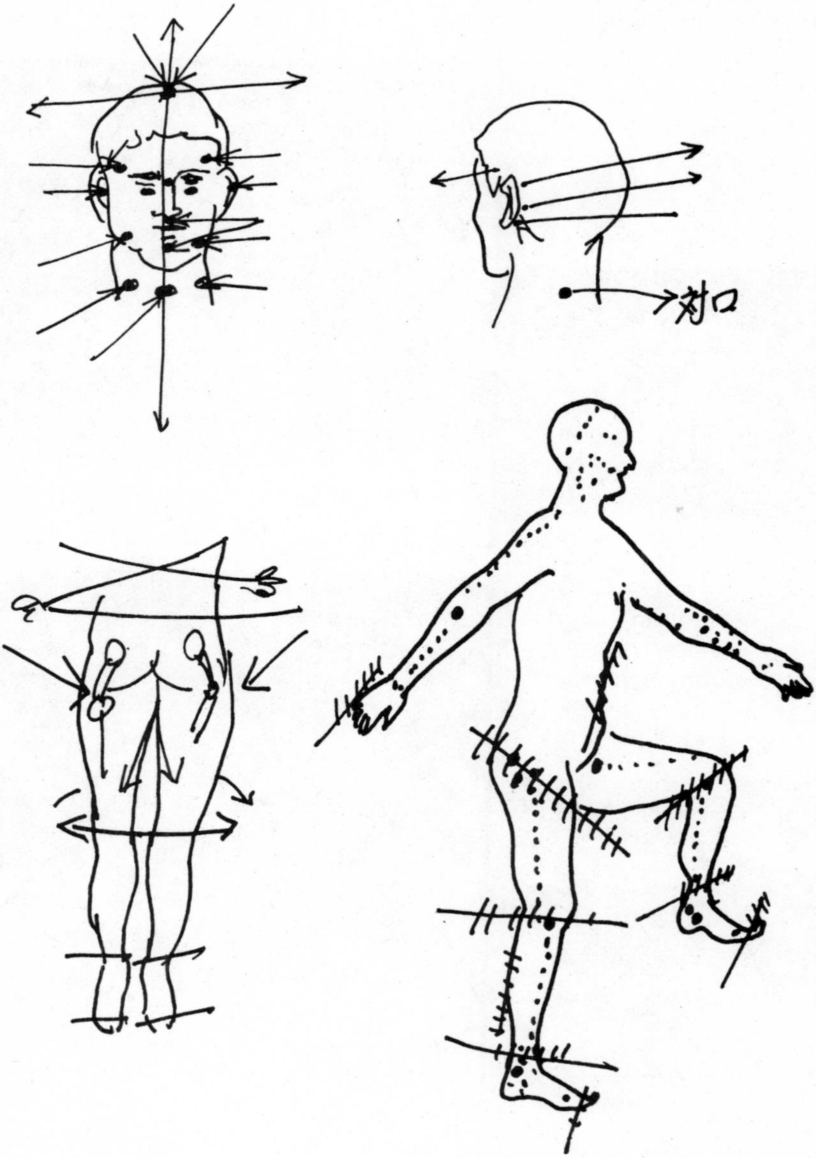

THE THREE CHARACTERISTICS AND FUNCTIONS OF KICKS

1. Hitting — to harm internally.
2. Snapping — speed-oriented from different directions. Rather than penetrating, these kicks are intended primarily to affect the outer or surface area of the body.
3. Thrusting — delivering a powerful force to an extremely small, well-focused target area.

STRAIGHT-LINE AND CIRCULAR ARC KICKS

For our purposes, there are basically two kinds of kicks: circular arc kicks which are made by swinging the leg outside the area occupied by your opponent in a round or circular motion and then bringing it back into alignment with a greater momentum than would otherwise be possible, and straight-line kicks which choose the straightest possible line between your foot and the target area of your opponent.

Because combat situations are always changing, no one can tell in advance which kick will be most effective in dealing with which situation. Applying any kick involves split-second decisions and excellent timing.

But, without being 100 percent true, it would be basically accurate to say that circular arc kicks, because of the greater distance they travel, are generally considered to be the more powerful. Straight-line kicks, because they do not span such distances, may be said to be faster—not faster in terms of the speed of the leg and foot at full extension, but faster in terms of the total time that elapses between your decision to kick and the arrival of your foot on target.

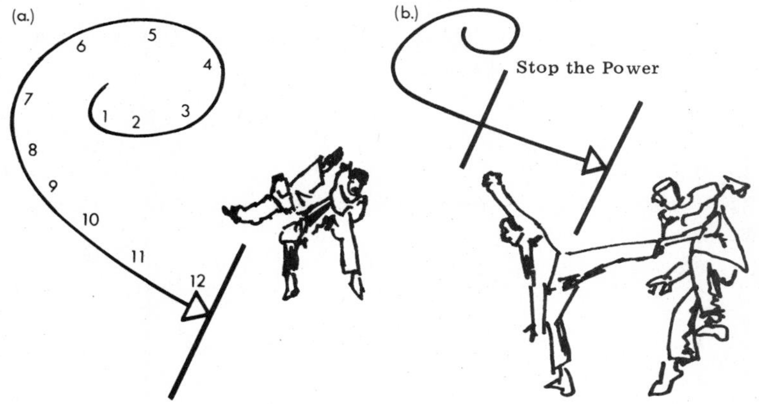

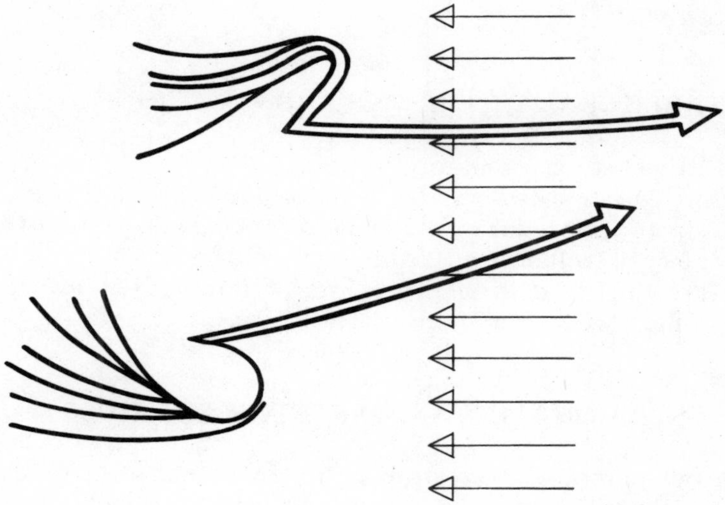

KICKING IN FREEFIGHTING

When fighting, to execute any kick properly, it is necessary to have both a clear view of the target area, and to be in the proper position.

Understandably, such a position is not offered freely by your opponent, but through practice, through learning how to shift your steps without leaving yourself open, you can maneuver yourself into the position of best advantage.

Executing kicks in forms competition often requires the martial artist to make the most of his coordination and gracefulness. In combat, obviously, some otherwise showy moves are abbreviated to the point of being nearly done away with. In competition, a kick that doesn't reach the selected target area has failed, regardless of how artful it looked.

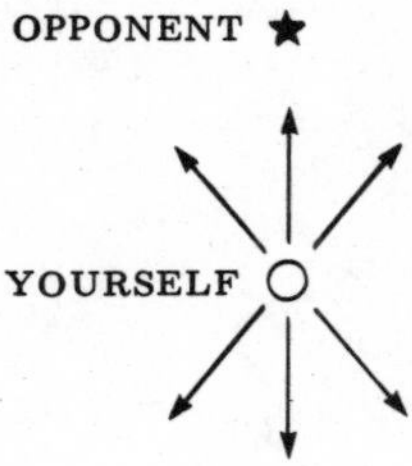

Remember: Forward and back are not the only directions you can move. Many attacks and defenses are most effective from oblique angles. You must decide on the basis of what you know about the strengths and weaknesses of yourself and your opponent.

TECHNIQUES BASIC TO ALL KICKS

My teaching experience convinces me that the typical novice is able to make use of only 10 to 20 percent of the power eventually available to him.

Having obtained the ability to deliver up to 100 percent of his available power, a well-trained student might be called capable of delivering truly "explosive kicks."

It should be remembered, too, that in freefighting it is sometimes possible to deliver more than 100 percent. Because it frequently becomes possible to exploit an opponent's reaction or momentum, it happens that an alert fighter may be able to strike with 200 or 300 percent of his ordinary force. As much as anything else, this is a matter of excellent timing, rhythm and speed.

If the kick is faster than the hand, which through constant training it can be, it is also capable of delivering five times as much power as the hand.

To assist you in an attempt to develop explosive kicks, it may be helpful to bear in mind the following equation:

Weight X Speed = Power

In other words, the lighter your bodyweight, the more speed required to develop a kick of equal force to the power generated by a slower but heavier fighter. The velocity of your kicks will ultimately depend on the elasticity of your body, the control of your breath, the accuracy of your aim and the single-mindedness of your concentration.

Although the flexibility of the ankle is a very important factor in determining kicking ability, the actual velocity of the kick is, perhaps more than anything else, determined by the power expended in the snap of the knee. But explosive kicking is not only done with the feet. Legs, waist, ankles, toes and hips are also important, and to the extent that you are able to incorporate and coordinate these elements into your kicks, they will take on added voltage.

● *Use Full Power Only At Full Extension*

Remember, tension not only hinders speed, but exhausts your strength. Many beginners tend to use full strength throughout the motion of striking. This is somewhat wasteful as well as unnecessary. While kicks should always be delivered at top speed, the entire leg should remain relaxed until the moment of full extension or just before contact, by which time full tension and muscle power should be concentrated in a powerful burst.

● *Raise the Kicking Leg and Knee Up High*

So that the execution of a variety of kicks can follow in one smooth motion, the knee should be raised as high as possible prior to flexing. There are a number of reasons for this:

1. The straighter the plane on which it travels, the more forceful the kick. In other words, the more the trajectory of your kick moves in a straight, horizontal line paralleling the floor, the more potent it will be. Imagine your foot as an arrow being delivered from your own waist level to the waist level of your opponent and you will understand the sense of this.
2. Kicking from such a high position allows your opponent less time to react. With the kick cocked high, it can shoot out to a wider variety of targets. Because of this, it becomes more difficult for your opponent to guess where you intend to strike him.
3. A kick thrown from a high position is harder to block. Driven up from the ground directly to the target, the kick can be stopped when your opponent lowers his forearm. Not knowing where you intend to kick him, and with your knee cocked high in the air, it will be much more difficult for your opponent to settle on how he will block the kick.

Further, the wise fighter will never begin with his kicking foot swept back towards the knee of his supporting leg (See page 24, photo 2, *Dynamic Kicks*). Having initially drawn the knee back, the kicker has nullified his opportunity to react speedily to his opponent. For example, consider the fighter faced with an opponent's oncoming head punch. Having spotted an opening to his opponent's rib cage, and hoping to deliver a side kick before his opponent's punch lands, the fighter cocks his knee wrongly and before he can raise his knee again to execute the kick, the opponent's punch connects. The fighter should have raised the knee of his kicking leg and shot his kick off from there. Then, even if his kick was too slow to land effectively, it would have acted as a block, halting the opponent's advance, and causing his punch to be ineffective.

● *Maintain A Straight Line Through the Body While Kicking*

Here the object is to make certain you invest more than just the muscular energy of your legs into your kicks. When the hips and whole body are thrust forward into the kick, tremendous power can result.

For example, imagine that you are delivering a side kick to a brick wall. The hip and extended leg are in line, but the body is not. The force of the kick is directed back towards you, and as at this point your trunk and legs are functioning as separate units, the kick will recoil off the brick wall and the shock of the recoil will necessarily be absorbed by your hip joint. As your trunk and leg are not aligned, your upper body will continue forward as the shock of your kick comes back at your hip joint. The power of such a kick is scattered and misdirected.

If, on the other hand, the entire body, hip and leg are held on the same line, the force of the blow will either break through the wall or repel you backwards. There will be no force to obstruct the full delivery of power. All your weight will be behind it.

● *Keep Sudden Changes in Movement and Rhythm to a Minimum*

Before and during the initiation of any kicking technique, the fighter's body should not undergo major changes in movement that will serve to help his opponent figure out where and when the next attack will arrive. If you are moving, continue to do so until the last instant. If you are still, continue still until the last instant. Only the leg should move at the start of the kick.

● *Use Eye Feints and Peripheral Vision*

The clever fighter soon becomes adept at watching his opponent's eyes for telltale signs of where the opponent will launch his attack, while learning tricks to disguise his own intentions. Also, learning to make use of his peripheral vision gives a fighter a wider range of awareness and enables him to spot possible openings for attack.

STRETCHING EXERCISES

KNEE BENDS

(1) Put your feet together and straighten your legs. (2) Begin your squat, still (3) holding hands over the knees. Now (4) straighten your legs while continuing to bend forward from the waist, and (5-7) force your knees to revolve in a counterclockwise direction so that you begin two connected motions: a motion involving squatting and standing, and a second revolving movement centered in the knees. Now (8), return to first position and continue, this time, revolving in a clockwise motion.

2

3

5

6

8

KNEE CIRCLES

(1) Assuming the same position as for the knee bend exercises, (2) place the palms of your hands on your knees and, (3) keeping your body as still as possible, (4) rotate your knees in counter and (5) clockwise circular motions 10 times.

2

3

5

1

2

3

JUMP SPLIT

(1) Put your feet together, extending your arms slightly and bending at the knees. (2) As your arms extend fully out and backward, all your weight should be shifted

VARIATION

to the balls of your feet. Now, (3) propel yourself upward, kicking your legs out straight, touching your fingertips to your toes.

ISOMETRIC EXERCISES

As illustrated by the accompanying photos, (1) elevate your leg to a bar placed about shoulder-height. (2&3) Press the heel of your foot against the bar as hard as you can for 10 seconds and tighten the muscles throughout your leg. (4) If no bar is available, use a partner to assist you as shown. Repeat procedure with other leg.

2

3

4

1

2

ALTERNATE SITTING KNEE STRETCH

(1) Sit on the floor with legs extending straight in front of you and feet together. (2) Holding on to your right foot and bending at the knee, bring your foot towards your abdomen and (3) place it across your fully extended left thigh as close to

3

the hip joint as possible. Now, bending from the waist, reach out and touch the toes of your left leg. (4) Having returned right leg to fully extended position, bend forward again touching both toes, and repeat exercise with opposite leg.

4

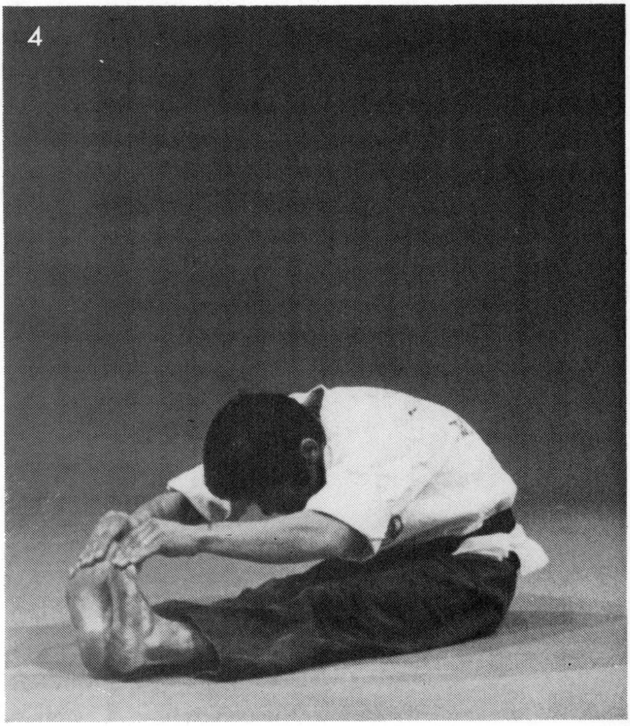

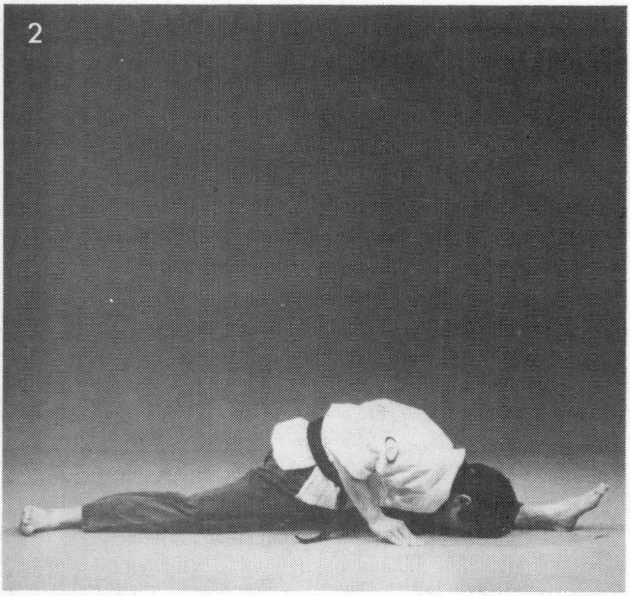

REVERSE SITTING HIP STRETCH

(1) Having settled slowly and gradually into a splits position, turn from the hips and bend forward until you can touch your forehead to the floor. (2) Then turn around and repeat exercise from the other side.

SQUATTING STRETCH

(1) Extend your right leg forward with your knee locked, bend at the left knee, squat down and fold your hands in front of your waist. Twist and bend forward at the hips. (2) Lift up from the waist, and using the muscles in both legs, raise yourself into (3) a position from which you can shift to the other side. (4) Again bend at the waist and lower your face as far as possible toward the floor. Exercise should be done in one continuous rocking motion, shifting from side to side, until back and leg muscles are fully relaxed.

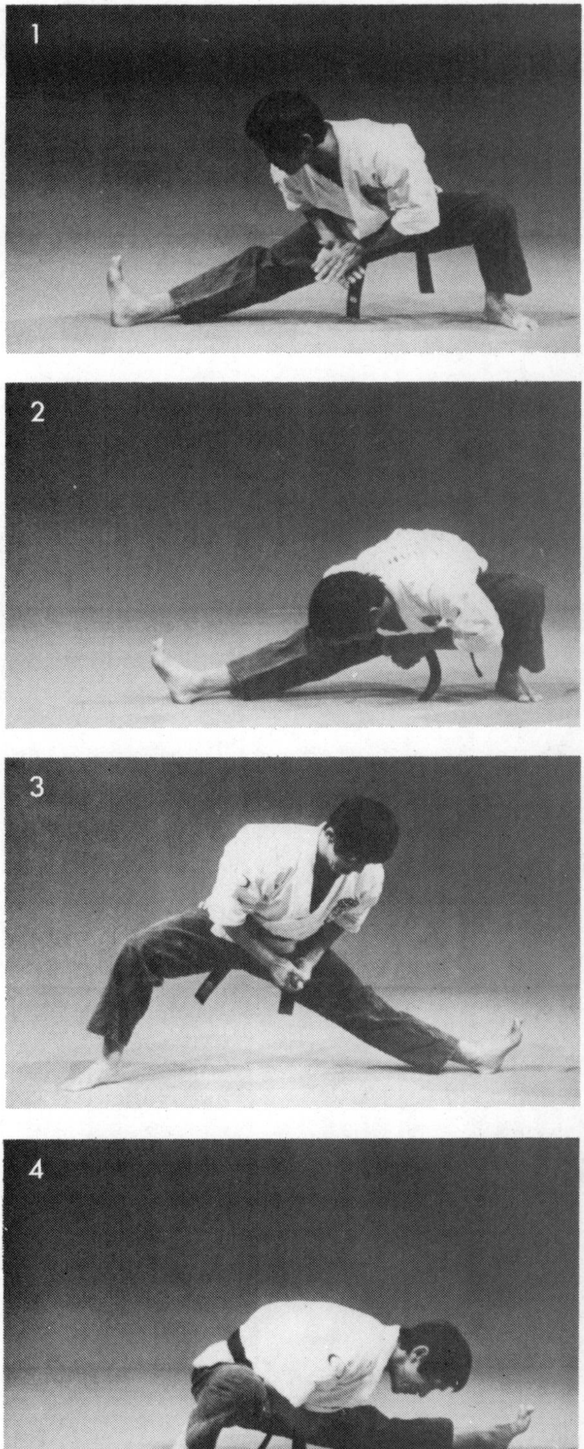

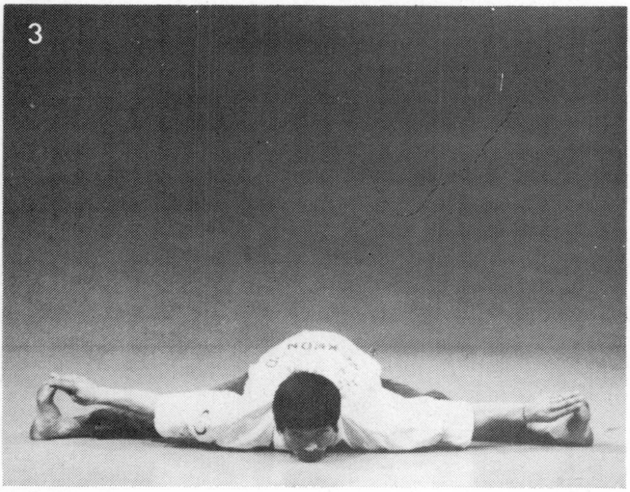

DOUBLE STRAIGHT LEG SPLITS STRETCH

(1) Having settled slowly and gradually into a splits position, lean forward until you can stretch your arms out and reach your toes. (2) Still holding your toes, bend forward from your hips until (3) your chin is touching the ground. Repeat this until the muscles in your back and legs are relaxed and loose.

DOUBLE BENT LEG SITTING STRETCH

(1) Sit on the floor, spread both legs, and press the soles of your feet together. (2) Lower your knees as far as possible, and keeping your back straight, lower your forehead until you can touch your feet. (3) Hold this position for about a minute.

DOWN
BACK UP BACK

(1) Take your position as shown in picture one. (2) Reach down to the floor in front of you by bending at the waist. Keep your knees locked and tighten the hamstring muscles. (3) Come up slightly then touch the floor between and in back of your legs. (4) Come up, put your hands on your waist, and (5) arch your back.

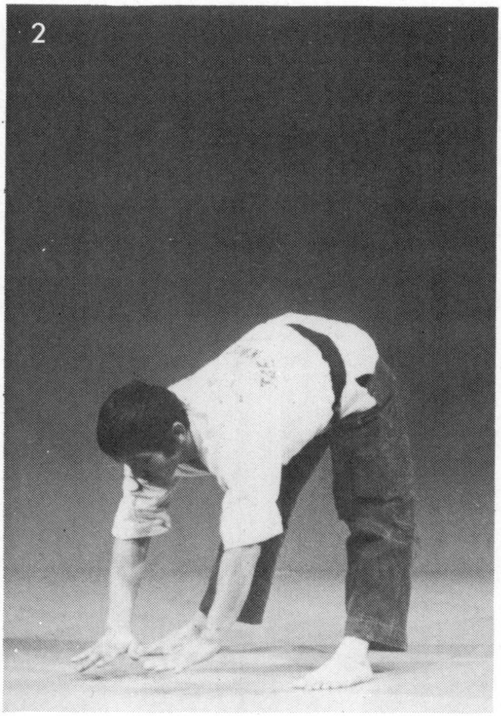
2

3

5

SITTING HAMSTRING STRETCH

(1) Take position as shown in picture. (2) Place your left hand around your right foot, and keeping your right leg in the original position, (3) extend your left leg, reaching across and

gripping your left kneecap with your right hand. (4) Stretch the leg straight out and up, while holding on to your knee, then (5) retract it and switch to the other leg.

SINGLE KICKS

In addition to going through the stretching exercises, it is also recommended that you practice the following kicks. Perform them slowly, at first, until you make sure you are doing everything right. Also, to develop the muscular strength for being able to use them in potential combat situations, practice holding the kicks in a "frozen" position at full extension for counts of 10, 20 and 30.

Some of these kicks differ slightly when they are used in forms competition. In some cases, it has seemed worthwhile to point out kick variations by discussing the different approaches. Whereas in forms a competitor is judged largely on intangibles such as grace, poise and smoothness of movement, in combat the object is to land kicks with quickness and power. Therefore, combat kicks tend to contain no flourishes or extra movements.

ANGULAR KICK

(1) Begin with your right leg forward and most of your weight on the left leg. (2-4) Shift your weight to the right forward leg, scoop your left foot in front of the right knee, and jump off on your right foot. (5) Your right leg continues and thrusts to full extension. In forms, your lower leg (the left) is held up in a cocked position. In competition, on the other hand, it is a good idea to let the non-kicking foot fall toward the floor. (6) At full extension, your entire right leg and the right side of your body are fully tensed. (7-10) As the tension releases, drop your left leg.

2

3

5

6

9

10

ANGULAR KICK
(in competition)

(A) Begin with your right foot forward and most of your weight on the left foot. Transfer weight to your right leg. (B) Shift weight to your forward leg, scoop your left foot in front of your right knee and jump off with your right leg so that it passes your left foot again. Your left foot is touching an invisible step. (C) Opponent unable to decide what kind of kick is coming at him. (D) As the kick reaches out for a full extension, lean your body back to adjust your distance. Your right hip is at full extension. The toes are curled back tightly, and your left knee is bent to help you retain proper balance. (E) As you straighten your left leg, your body bounces back up. (F) Return to position.

HATCHET KICK

(1) Lift your leg as though you were executing an inside crescent kick. (2) Once the kick reaches its peak, lean backwards so that it can be powered with the back muscles, and drop your heel straight down into opponent's face.

360-DEGREE HATCHET KICK

(1) Start by facing opposite directions. (2) As your opponent makes his move, quickly transfer your weight to your right leg and (3) bring your left knee up high towards your opponent and block as needed. (4) Leading with your right elbow and hip, start a clockwise spin. Your right heel should come up off the floor as you turn. (5) Still spinning, jump off with the right leg, and (6) lift it as high in the air as possible. (7&8) As your left leg touches down, your right foot comes straight down at your opponent. Put your waist into it and jerk your shoulder to pack the kick with speed and power.

2

3

5

6

8

JUMPING BACK ROUNDHOUSE

(1) Start with right foot forward. (2) Jump up off the ground as you turn counterclockwise. (3) Bring your left knee up; then follow with the right knee. Both hands should be used like levers to power and speed the

spin. (4) Increasing your momentum, tense both hands and curl back toes before striking the target. (5) Bring your left hip back towards the left shoulder and thrust your right foot in toward your target.

SPIN BACK ROUNDHOUSE

(1) Begin with your left leg forward with most of your weight on your right leg. (2&3) Pivot clockwise 180 degrees and snap your head around and over your right shoulder to watch the target. (4) As your right leg moves toward your opponent, your body is turned completely around with most of your weight on the left leg. (5-8) Check your opponent to make sure he is still hesitating. Immediately raise your right knee (which is your defensive block), and follow up to the target with your leg muscles fully tensed. Do not bring foot back until you have reached your target.

2

3

5

6

8

TURNING BACK ROUNDHOUSE KICK

(1) Begin with your right foot back. (2-4) Turn clockwise, showing opponent your left heel. Use your arms and shoulders to help you spin. As your head whirls and you can see your opponent by looking over your right shoulder, transfer your weight to the ball of your left foot. (5) As right elbow turns out, start raising right leg. Concentrate on lifting the knee as high as possible. (6&7) Direct your kick from the side, leading and striking with the edge of your right foot. The muscles in your right leg and the entire right side of your body are completely tensed. (8-10) Release your tension and start to draw the kick back. Kick is withdrawn from the knee. The knee is still held in a defensive position. Lower the leg and reassume your original stance.

1

4

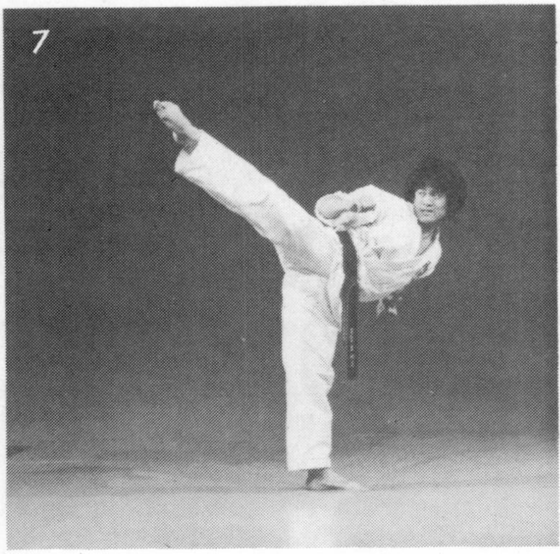
7

8

2

3

5

6

9

10

TURNING BACK ROUNDHOUSE KICK (in competition)

(A) Begin with left leg forward. (B) Transfer your weight to your right leg and start leaning back. (C) Turn your body to trick opponent into thinking you are throwing a back kick. (D) The more you turn, the lighter your right foot becomes—the more of your weight is assumed by the ball of the left foot. (E&F) Although your leg points at opponent's stomach, he still is not certain what sort of kick you are about to throw. To further confuse him, drive toward his stomach. Before reaching the stomach, throw kick to the outside, from a different direction than he's expecting. (G) As kick is being delivered, spin arms in a counterclockwise direction. When the kick lands, because of the counter-motion started by the right arm, you will have 100 percent balance on impact.

B

D

E

G

DEFENSE TURNING BACK HOOK KICK

(1&2) Start facing opposite directions. Making sure that he cannot kick you and that it is too far for him to reach you with a punch, lift your left leg and place your foot on your opponent's knee. (3) Leading with your right elbow and hip, start a clockwise spin, raising your right heel as you turn. Still whirling, shift your weight to your

right foot, then jump off from it. (4) As your body continues to move clockwise, extend your right leg in a circular arc, hitting with the back of your heel or the ball of your foot, while making sure to keep your toes pointing forward. (5) Land on your left leg as your right leg continues its clockwise descent.

SPIN-BACK JUMPING ROUNDHOUSE KICK

(1) Start with your left leg drawn back. (2-5) Shift your weight to the right leg. Starting with the left elbow, wheel counterclockwise, bending the shoulder and following with the waist. Then jump off. The moment you leave the ground, allow your left leg to revolve counterclockwise, then follow with the right leg directly after. Once in the air, jerk your hips toward your target, and extend your right leg to the striking area while turning with the shoulders. (6) At full extension, bring right arm back in a clockwise direction while kicking. Release all tension. (7-9) As the right leg retracts, land on the left. Lower your right leg to original stance.

2

3

5

6

8

9

360-DEGREE SPIN HOOK

(1&2) Begin with your left leg back and transfer your weight from your left to your right leg. (3) As your left leg comes up off the ground, start turning your body simultaneously. Your muscles must be relaxed until you begin to jump. (4) Having jumped as high as you can, bring your legs together and spin your body as fast as possible. (5) As your body continues the clockwise motion, (6) extend your leg with toes pointing. At full extension, the entire upper part of both shoulders and the calves of your legs should be fully tensed with your toes pointing as hard as they can. (7) As your right leg begins to fall, (8) twist your right hip down and back, making sure your foot still points at your opponent, until you are (9) back where you started.

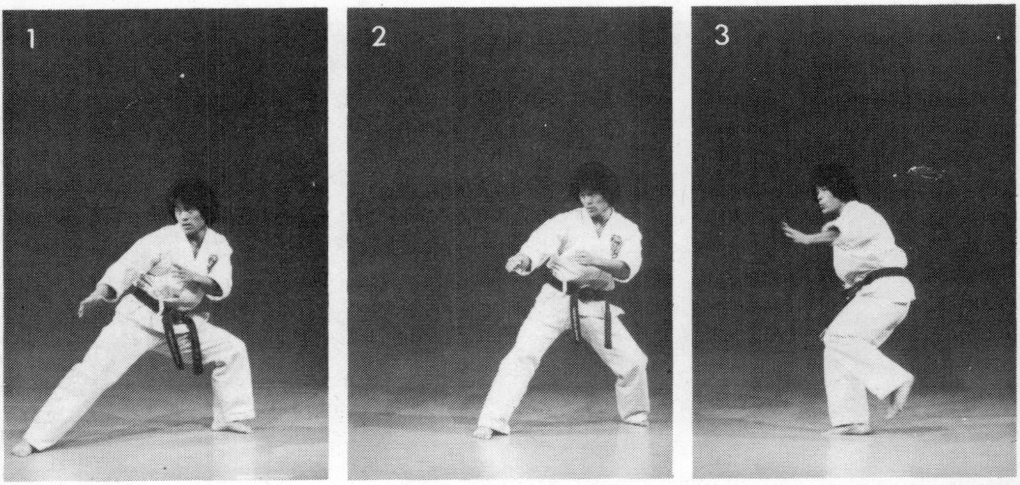

FRONT VIEW

4
5
6
7
8
9

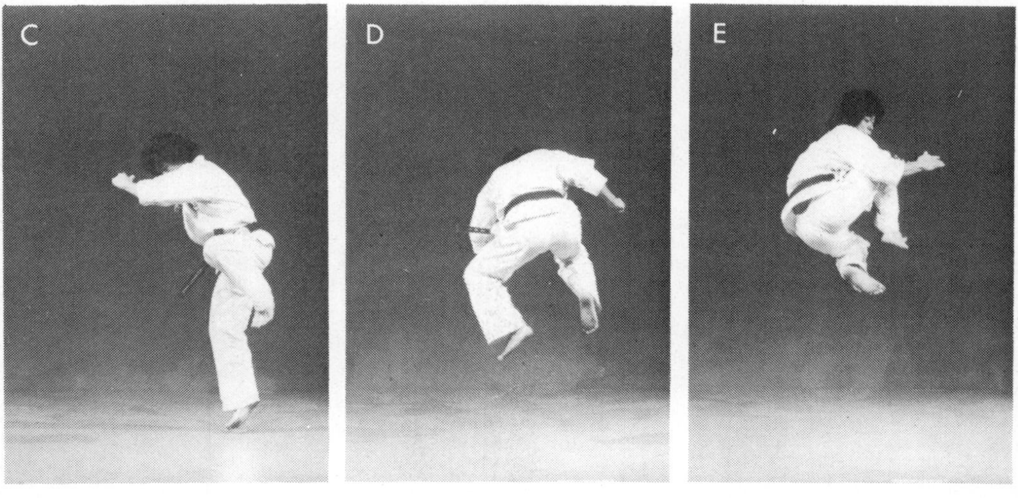
C
D
E

JUMPING BACK KICK

***Use this kick as a counterattack when both you and your opponent are facing the same direction.

(1&2) As opponent launches his attack, prepare to execute a back kick, being careful not to telegraph your intention to your opponent. (3) Block as necessary. (4) Jump off on both feet, using your upper torso to

spin your body clockwise, and keeping your knees bent with your feet tucked up. (5&6) As your right side nears the target, extend your right leg in a thrusting motion, striking opponent with the back of your right heel. When fully extended, the entire right side of your back and right leg are filled with tension.

JUMPING ROUNDHOUSE KICK

(1) Start with the left leg back and with most of your weight on the left leg. (2&3) Shift your weight to your forward leg. (4) Scoop your left foot in front of your right knee and turn your right shoulder into your opponent, pulling your left shoulder back. Jump off with your left leg. (5) As you jump off, turn your right hip into your opponent and your leg so that the right leg passes your left foot again. Your left foot has touched the invisible step. (6) Led by your right hip, your right leg continues and thrusts to full extension. In forms, the lower leg (in this case, the left leg) should be held in a cocked position. In competition, however, it is a good idea to extend the nonkicking foot towards the floor as demonstrated here in the step-by-step sequence. At full extension, your entire right leg and the muscles in your left lower back are completely tensed. (7) Release your tension in order to keep your balance after falling. (8) Bring your right foot back, keeping your knee high as you are dropping onto your left leg. (9) Notice that the upper part of the body has been trying to maintain the same position after the full extension of the kick.

2

3

5

6

8

9

JUMPING
ROUNDHOUSE KICK
(in competition)

2

4

5

7

1

JUMPING FRONT HOOK

(1) Begin with your right foot forward. (2&3) Push slightly with your left leg, and as your left foot skips towards your right, jump off with the right leg. (4) Tucking your left foot up beneath you, cock your right leg near the right side of your chest—high and parallel to the ground. (5&6) Extend your right leg upwards in a circular arc while arching your back. Drop your right shoulder backwards to hook your kick across. At full extension, concentrate 100 percent on your toe. (7&8) Your left leg should be reaching for the ground. Land on your left leg as your right leg retracts. Keep the right leg high for your defense. (9) Return to beginning position.

4

7

2

3

5

6

8

9

1

JUMPING HOOK KICK

(1) Start with both of you facing the same direction. (2&3) As your opponent throws his kick, move slightly back, or duck down until he reaches his full extension. (4) You now find him retracting his kick and can see that his knee is not up high; so you know that he will not throw another kick. Transfer your weight to the front slightly. (5) Once his foot is down on the ground, take an invisible step with the left leg, and jump up with the right leg so it passes your left foot. Notice that your left foot is facing opponent's front leg to prevent him from kicking with his right leg. (6&7) Bring your left hip back, tuck your left foot up beneath you, cock your right leg upwards, and extend the kick in a circular arc while arching your back. Drop your right shoulder backwards to hook your kick across back of opponent's head. Your left leg should be reaching for the ground. Land on your left leg. (8) Finding yourself in this position, bring your legs together and (9) shift your weight to your left leg, then (10-12) launch a back kick to your opponent's groin area.

4

7

10

2

3

5

6

8

9

11

12

360-DEGREE HOOK KICK

(1) Start with your right foot forward. (2) As your opponent makes a move, quickly transfer your weight to your right leg. (3) Jump off the right leg, spinning clockwise and blocking as becomes necessary. (4) Continue to spin and rise. (5) As you turn, keep your knees bent and your feet tucked up. (6&7) As the bottom of your foot faces your opponent, try to keep your right leg, which is bent, parallel to the ground. At full extension, the right foot is tensed and the right side of your back is arched tightly. About the time extension is completed, allow your left foot to drift down to the floor.

2

4

5

7

ROLLING HILL KICK

(1) This kick is used as counterattack. If you see that an opponent's attack will be high, lower your left shoulder and bend your left leg. (2) Roll forward, making sure you tuck your chin on your shoulder. (3&4) Once you find yourself on your shoulder, bring your left foot to your thigh, right foot arching toward his face. (5) Straighten your back to extend your kick. (6) Jerk your back and tighten your chest. (7) Make sure your foot is followed down along with your opponent's body. Strike his solar plexus with your heel.

1

3

6

2

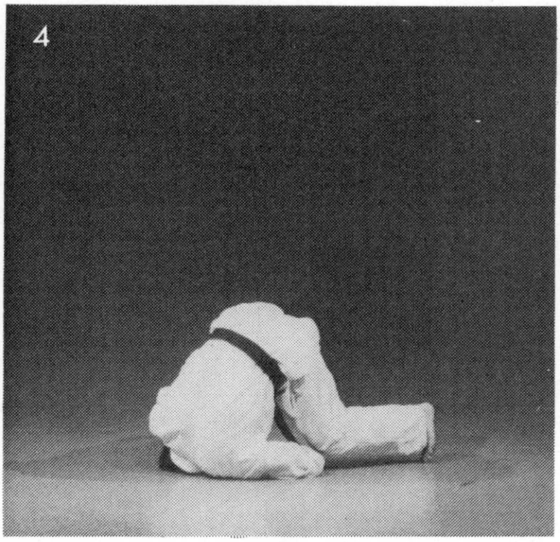
4

5

7

ROLLING HILL KICK
(in competition)

B

C

E

F

I

J

ROUNDHOUSE HOOK

(1) Start with your left leg forward. (2&3) Twist your upper body to the left as though you were throwing a right punch. (4) Move your right hip forward as you bring the right knee up in front of you. Brush the right foot closely past the left leg. (5) Allowing your knee to be high, twist the right hip left and downwards in a snapping motion as you extend your leg. Arch your back and bring your foot up in an arc. (6) At full extension, the muscles of your right leg and throughout the right side of the back should be completely tensed. (7) Turn your head over your right shoulder in order to keep an eye on your opponent. (8) Releasing the tension, hook to your right, bringing your left shoulder forward slightly to increase the power of the kick. (9) Prepare to kick again if necessary.

2

3

5

6

8

9

ROUNDHOUSE HOOK
(against two opponents)

B
C
E
F
I
J

COMPLEX KICKS

DOUBLE HOOK KICK

(1) When attacked from both sides, start with your right foot back. Turn your left hip and shoulder in front of you. (2) Transfer your weight to the left leg, lifting your right, and bringing it back in behind your left. The right heel and the ball of your left foot nearly touch, for the further apart they are, the less power you will be able to deliver in the kick. Concentrating on the intensity and the force you want to go into the kick, open your hands and tighten the muscles in your fingers as though you could lift yourself from the floor with your arms. (3) Draw your left knee up high towards the right side of your chest, and as you do so, pivot clockwise on your supporting leg, throwing the bottom of your left foot towards the target. (4) Your

kick has arrived in an arcing motion. At this moment, jerk your left hip and shoulder to the left so that your foot travels up and across to the target. At full extension, the back of your left leg and the left side of your back should be fully tensed. (5) Continue hooking and locate your left leg behind your right foot. Glance to your right to focus on the other target. (6) Push slightly with your left leg, and as your left foot skips towards your right, jump off from your right leg. Extend your right leg upwards in a circular arc and arch your back. (7) Drop your left shoulder backwards to hook your kick across. As kick is nearing full extension, the left leg should be reaching for the ground.

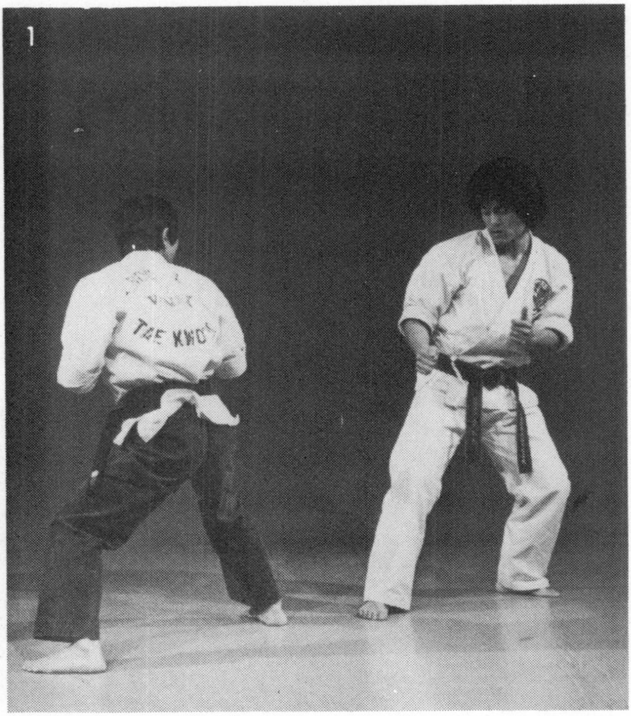

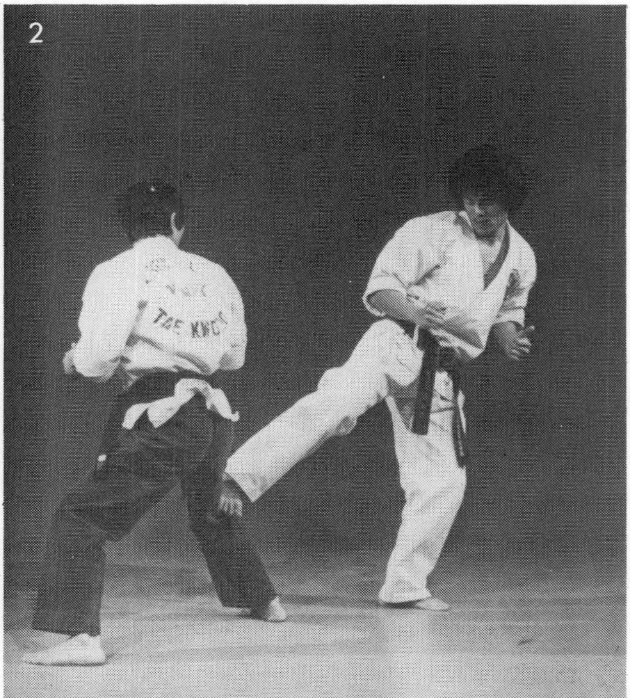

SIDE KICK WITH ROUNDHOUSE KICK

(1) Start by facing opposite directions. (2) Shifting your weight as little as possible, lift your right knee up, and shoot your kick out straight to the side, leading with the edge of your right foot. The momentum of the lift and kick, done in a single motion, will slide you towards the target. Be sure to hold the edge of your right foot parallel to the ground. Firmly push or kick the side of opponent's knee until you see it bending. (3) Once his knee is collapsing, his body will start to

fall. At this moment, move your right foot towards the target. (4) Keeping your knee high, twist your right hip left and down in a snapping motion as you extend your leg. Arch your back and bring your foot up in an arc. At full extension, the muscles in your right leg are tensed and the right side of your back is arched tightly. (In competition, this is not necessary; instead, have a fast snap.) At full extension, turn your face over your right shoulder.

FRONT SIDE WITH SIDE KICK

(1) Begin with your right foot back. (2) Turn your right shoulder towards opponent as though you were prepared to throw a reverse punch. Turn the right hip and lift kicking foot off the ground. (3) Right hip turns more and more sharply as the knee is lifted higher. Cock your toes backwards, so that the ball of your kicking foot faces your target. (4&5) As the right leg is extended, tighten the muscles of your supporting leg; however, as you near full extension, the muscles in your right leg should begin to relax, maintaining their rigidity only about the supporting ankle. The muscles on the right side of your stomach should be fully tensed. (6) Bring kick back. As shown by photo, the left shoulder is still not brought forward. (7) Turn your head in and to the right, and lean back and to the left with the upper part of your body. (8) As kick is being delivered, your hip should be approximately where your knee was in picture seven. With foot pointed outward to strike with the outside edge, continue and strike target. (9) At full extension, the muscles of your right leg, and along the entire right side of back and buttocks, are completely tensed. (10) Having released all tension from the first kick, jump hard off your supporting leg, and look to your left. (11) Cock right foot beneath you, turning its sole upward. (12) At the peak of your jump, lean backward and extend kick out. At full extension, the left side of your back should be tightly arched. Snap power into kick.

2

3

5

6

8

9

11

12

FRONT SIDE
WITH SIDE KICK
(against two opponents)

B

D

E

G

H

J

HOOK KICK FROM FRONT KICK POSITION

(1) Front kick has been thrown. (2) Draw right hip back. (3) Relax as you pull back your kick. (4) Without a break in motion, while foot is still in the air, turn upper trunk counterclockwise, and bring your right knee high under the right side of your chest. Swing your kicking foot up in an arcing motion. (5) As your right leg extends, jerk your right hip and shoulder to the right,

pulling your kick back towards your shoulder in a circular arc. At full extension, the muscles in the back of the right leg and the muscles in the right side of your lower leg, add power to the hooking motion of the kick. (6) Continue this powerful snapping hook until your leg is tucked back in a cocked position. At this point your right foot should still be tensed.

FRONT KICK WITH JUMPING HOOK KICK

(1) Begin with right foot forward. (2) Twist your upper body to the right. (3) Bring your knee up high toward the left side of your chest, brushing it closely by your supporting leg. (4&5) As kicking leg extends, tighten the muscles of your supporting leg, and turn left hip forward. At full extension, the muscles along the left side of your stomach are fully tensed, as is the back of your supporting leg. (6) Pull kick back from hip, muscles in leg should be fully relaxed. (7)

(CONTINUED)

(CONTINUED)

(CONTINUED)

Turn your left shoulder counterclockwise, and throw a right punch. (8) Immediately pull your left hip back and jump off from a sideways position. Tuck your left foot up beneath you, cocking your right leg up near the right side of your chest, keeping it high and nearly parallel to the ground. Drop your right shoulder backwards and hook your kick across. (9) Release tension. (10) Land on your left leg as your right leg retracts. (11) Lower your right leg to its original position.

8

9

11

FRONT KICK WITH SIDE KICK

(1) Begin with your left leg forward. (2) Twist your upper body as if throwing a right punch. (3) Use this momentum to move your right knee forward, keeping it high and to the right side of your chest. Bring your left shoulder to the left and rear. As you draw leg upwards, remember that it should brush closely against your left leg. Left leg is still bent. (4) As your right leg extends, tighten the muscles in your supporting leg, and turn your right hip forward. (5) At full extension, the muscles of your supporting leg, and all along the back of your supporting leg, are fully tense. Think of this as though you were trying to support, very briefly, all your weight on the ball of the supporting foot. (6) Release tension, and use your hips to pull your leg back, keeping your knee high. Turn your foot into the side kick position. (7) Pivot further to the

(CONTINUED)

2

3

5

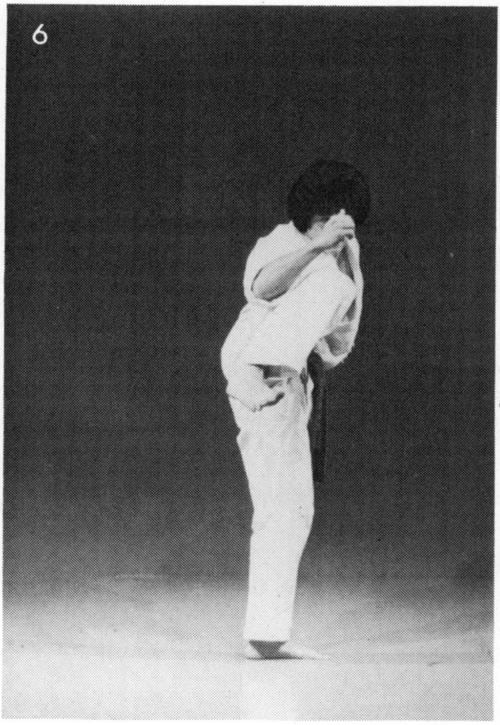

6

(CONTINUED)

(CONTINUED)

(CONTINUED)

right on your supporting leg, turning your right knee over so that your right foot, leading edge first, may continue its straight path. (8&9) At full extension, the muscles in your right leg, and throughout the right side of your lower back and buttocks, are completely flexed. (10) Release tension, and bring your stance to its original position by withdrawing right foot back along the path it traveled. (11-13) Remember to keep your knee high. All your weight remains on your left leg, and you are ready to throw another kick if necessary.

8

9

12

13

FRONT KICK WITH JUMPING BACK KICK

(1) Begin with your right leg forward, and twist upper trunk as if throwing a left punch. (2&3) Bring your left knee forward and lift it high and to the left side of your chest. As it rises, brush it closely against the supporting leg. (4) Extending the left leg, tighten the muscles of the supporting leg, and turn the left hip forward. (5) With leg fully extended, the muscles on your right side, including those of the stomach and of the supporting leg, should be fully flexed. (6) Bring your hip back to return the kick. Leg muscles should be completely relaxed. (7) Turn your head to the rear. (8) Making use of the strength in your shoulders, whirl and jump off. (9) Sole turned upward, cock your left foot. Lean forward and kick right leg out horizontally. The right side of kicking leg is tightly arched, and the right heel is turned up slightly.

2

3

5

6

8

9

FRONT KICK
WITH JUMPING BACK KICK
(in competition)

B

D

E

G

FRONT KICK, WITH JUMPING ROUNDHOUSE KICK

(1) Begin with your right leg forward. (2) Twist your upper body to the left as if you were throwing a left punch. (3) Move your left knee forward and lift it high to the left side of your chest. As it comes up, it should brush closely against the supporting leg. (4) Extending your right leg, tighten the muscles of the support-

ing leg, and turn the right hip forward. After the kick, release your tension and use your hips to pull your left leg back as you are returning to original stance. (5) Before your left leg is fully back, jump up from the foot you are standing on. (6) Twist your waist and body and throw your roundhouse kick out.

DOUBLE SIDE KICK

(1) When facing opposite directions, shift the weight of your body as little as possible, and lift the right knee up along the right side of your body. (2) Shoot your kick out straight to the side, leading with the edge of your right foot. (3) As the momentum of your first kick slides you in toward your target, concentrate on delivering both kicks with the same motion and holding the edge of your kicking foot parallel to the ground. (4&5) As your opponent begins to collapse, bring kicking leg up in a straight line to strike again with a higher kick. (6) At full extension, the muscles of the right leg and the muscles through the entire right side and buttocks are completely tensed. (7) Release tension and simply draw back with right leg. The major concern about the second kick has been to bring the kicking foot up and out in a straight line. (8) Continue to hold your knee high as your body progresses back to an upright position. (9) On finding yourself again with both feet on the ground, prepare for a counterattack—just in case.

2

3

5

6

8

9

ROUNDHOUSE DROP SPIN BACK KICK

(1) Begin with your right leg back. (2) With most of your weight on your right leg, shift your weight as little as possible, and shoot your kick out straight to the side. The momentum of the lift and kick, executed with a single motion, will slide you in towards your target—your opponent's front leg. (3) Having released tension with the side kick, lower your kicking leg to the ground, allowing the left foot to remain forward. (4) Shift most of your weight to the right leg, pivot clockwise 180 degrees, while still keeping close watch over your target. (5) Drop left knee to the ground. (6) Snap head around so as to be able to look back over the right shoulder. (7) Pull your left

(CONTINUED)

(CONTINUED)

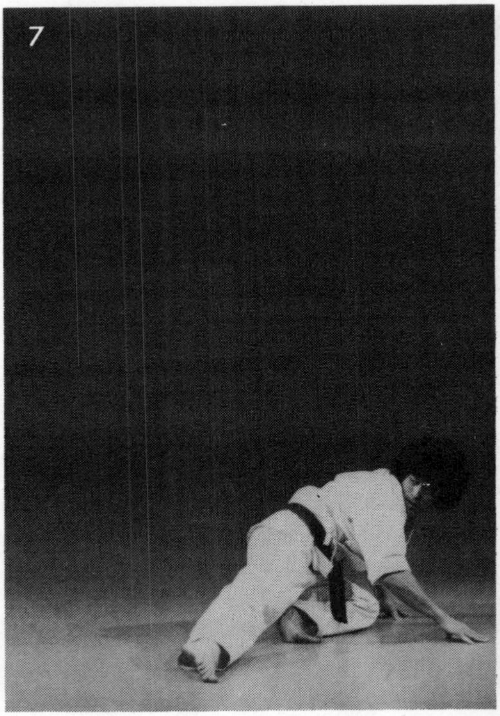

(CONTINUED)

knee toward your chest while extending your right leg in a clockwise arc. The instant your right leg goes out, drop your hands to the floor as necessary to support yourself. (8) Support areas are: the left knee, the ball of that foot, and, if necessary, both hands. During full extension of the kick, your right buttock is completely tensed. (9) As your right leg continues to arc, bend that knee and place the ball of the right foot on the floor behind you. Your left knee should begin to lift up from the floor. (10&11) Using this momentum and your left hand for assistance, lean forward and rise to your original stance. The swinging of your right hand from its position on the floor to the right side of your body, should give you extra lift.

SITTING KICKS

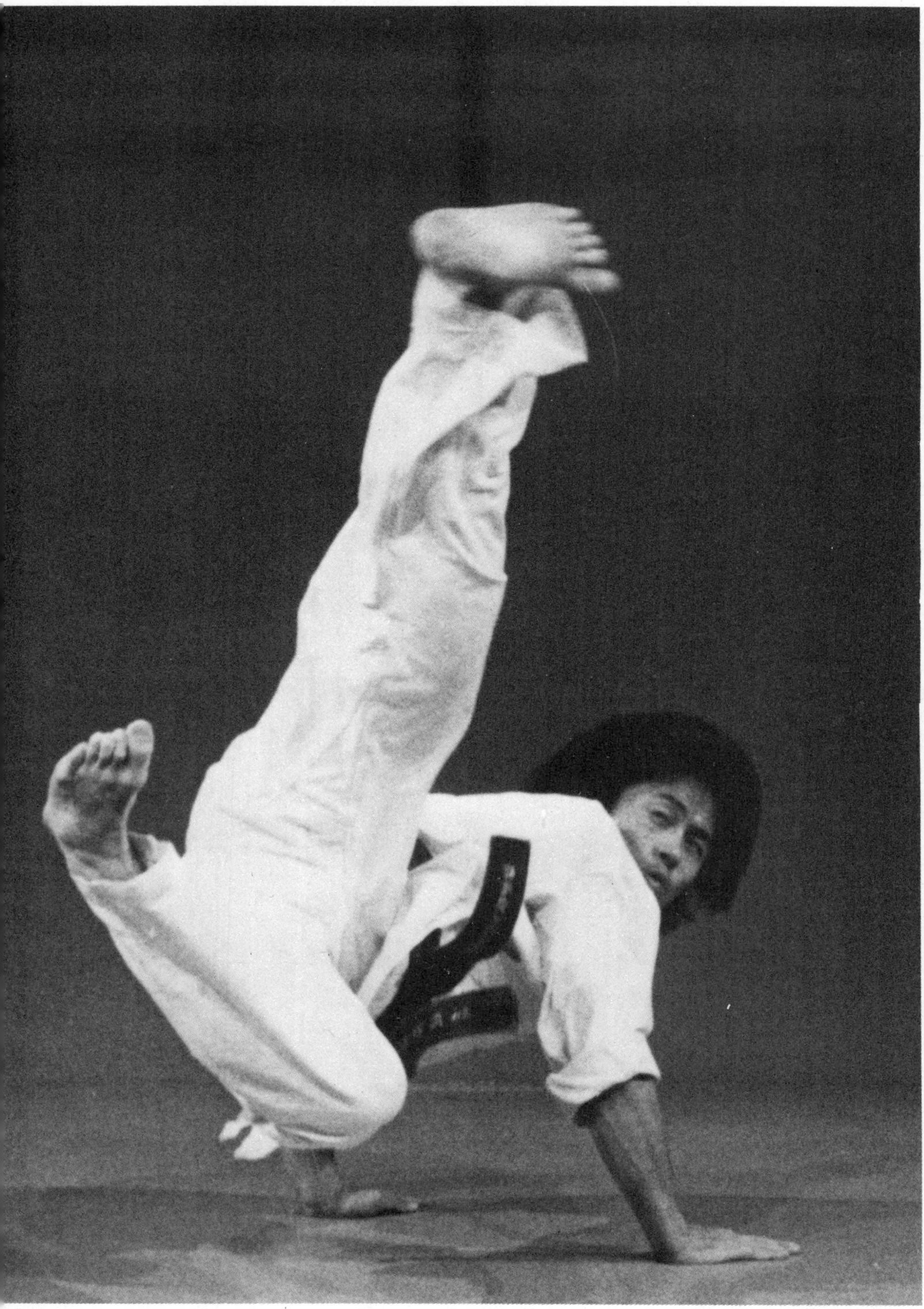

SITTING FRONT KICK

(1) Sit down as in picture with the palms of your hands on the ground and fingers pointing back. (2) Lift your buttocks up and bring your left knee up high towards your chest. (3) As your left leg extends, tighten the muscles of your supporting leg, and turn your left hip forward. (4) At full extension, the muscles on the right side of your stomach and the back of your supporting leg are fully tensed. (5-7) Release your tension and lower your hips as you pull your kick back to your sitting position.

2

3

6

7

SITTING SIDE KICK

(1) Sit down as in picture with the palms of your hands on the ground and fingers pointing back. (2&3) Turn your body completely to your left and bring your right hand over to your left-hand side. At this time, your right knee is rising up. (4) Bring your right knee forward and prepare to kick. (5) As your right leg extends, watch your opponent. (6) At full extension, the right side of your back should be tightly arched—right leg, too. (7-10) Release the tension in the kick, then lower your hips to your original position.

2

3

5

6

9

10

SITTING ROUNDHOUSE

(1) Sit down as in picture with the palms of your hands on the ground and fingers pointing back. (2&3) Turn your body completely to your left and bring your right hand over to your left-hand side. At this time, your right knee is rising up. (4) As your right leg extends, tighten the muscles of the thigh on your kicking leg. (5) At full extension, with your weight on your supporting knee, look over to your right shoulder to your target area. (6-8) Release your tension and lower your hips while drawing the kick back to your sitting position.

2

3

5

6

8

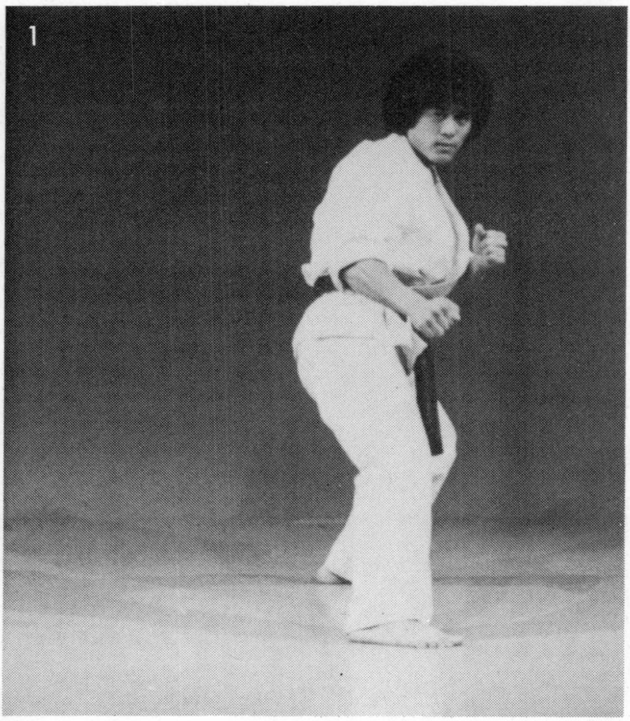

DROP SIDE KICK

(1) Begin with your right foot forward. (2) As you drop down, cock your right knee near your right shoulder, so that you are supporting yourself primarily on your hands and right knee. (3) Fire the side kick, making sure that it travels in a straight line. At full extension, the muscles in

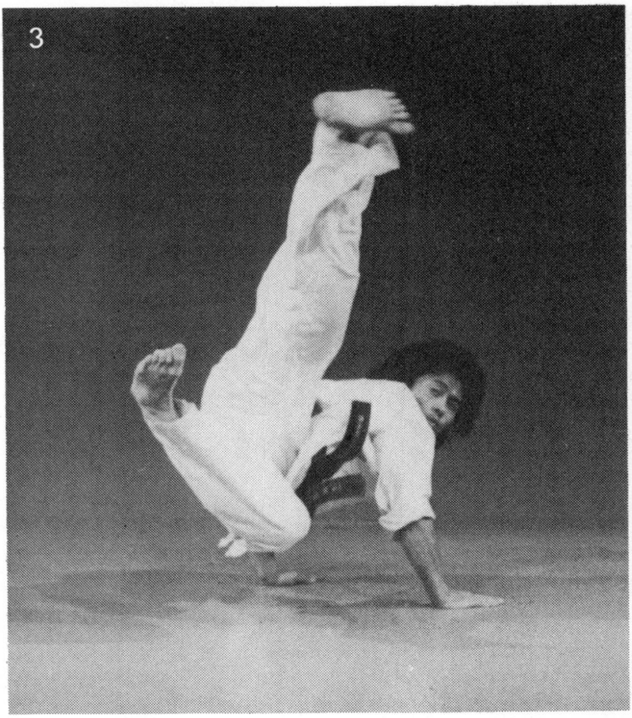

your right leg, your shoulders and the entire right side of your lower back and buttocks should be completely tensed. Hands and arms must support your weight. (4) Release your tension, allowing the force of gravity to help lower the kicking leg.

TAKE DOWNS

TAKE DOWN I

(1) For offensive and defensive use when you and your opponent are facing opposite directions. (2-4) Block the punches coming towards your head. (5) Moving in, pull your left leg up behind your right, and lift right leg while securing a good grip on the upper part of your opponent's body. (6) Your calf should land against the back of his knee. (7) Push him with your right arm, while sweeping against the back of his knee in the opposite direction. (8-10) Once your opponent is off the ground, hang on to him with your right to insure complete control of him. (11) Maneuver him into the desired position. (12) Strike him.

2

3

5

6

8

9

11

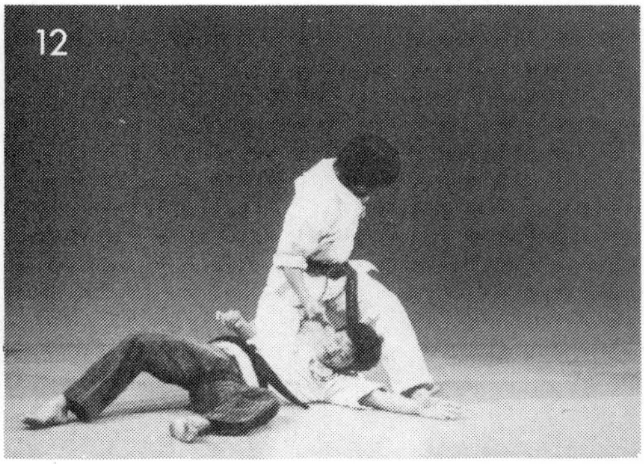
12

TAKE DOWN II

(1-3) For use when both you and your opponent are facing the same direction. Opponent is delivering a kick. (4) Move a little closer towards him without altering your stance. (5&6) The upper part of your body (chest and head) should be moving in the same direction as opponent's kick to prevent it from landing. Notice that your left hand is underneath his kick and your right hand is over it. (7) Now turn your right hip, pivoting your body counter-clockwise. (8) Hang on to him with both hands, locating him wherever you want him to be on the ground. (9) Let go with your left hand to punch him.

2

3

5

6

8

9

SCISSOR KICK TAKE DOWN

(1) Begin with right foot forward and most of your weight on your left leg. (2) Shift your weight to your forward leg, scoop your left foot behind your right leg and jump off with your right leg. The left foot is touching an invisible step. (3) While you are jumping into your opponent, make sure your right leg is in a position to land on his stomach. Your left leg should be behind his two legs. (4) As your body falls, tighten your legs. (5) Now you begin to take him down, sweeping with the left leg from the back, and pushing him with the right leg from the front. (6) Continue to exert force. (7) For more power, use the muscles of your midsection. Leave your right leg down so he won't be able to get up. (8) Your left leg is still sweeping upwards. (9) Throw a heel kick to his groin or stomach.

1

4

7

2

3

5

6

8

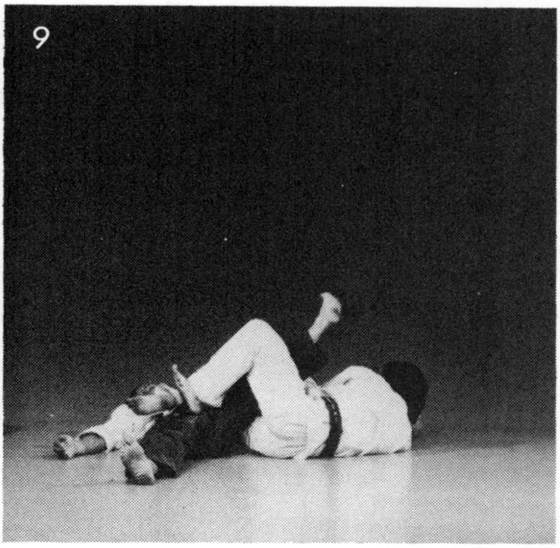
9

SPIN BACK SCISSOR KICK

(1-4) Standing with your right leg forward, block opponent's kick lightly. After blocking opponent's punch, most of your weight should be on your back leg as you seek for the target area. (5) Taking hold of opponent's arm, draw your right up and forward in an arcing motion, moving your right hip slightly forward as you bring the kicking knee up in front of you. (6) Twist your right hip to the left and down in a snapping motion as you extend your kick. (7) Retract your kick along the same path while remembering to keep your knee high. (8)

(CONTINUED)

2

4

5

7

(CONTINUED)

(CONTINUED)

(CONTINUED)

Drop your right foot behind his front leg with your heel up. Your right hand still holds fast to his arm. (9) When your right knee nears the ground you may let go with your right hand. Immediately drop hand to the ground for support. Now all your weight is balanced on your right hand and leg. (10) Turn your left shoulder back to help with the spin. Your knee is now touching the ground. (11) Your left leg heel-kicks his stomach directly from the ground. (12) Your right leg continues to sweep his front leg forward as the force of your kick continues to bring about his collapse. (13) Lock him with your left foot and bring your right leg up, making sure that your heel is pointing towards the ceiling. (14) Your heel strikes his stomach.

9

11

12

14

DEFENSE-AGAINST-TWO KICK

(1-4) As the kick comes from your right, catch it with your right hand as shown in the picture. With your left hand, catch the kick that comes from your left. (5) Transfer your weight to your right leg. (6) Bring your left leg to your right leg. At the same time, locate your right leg behind the right side of your opponent's supporting leg. (7) Turn your whole body to the right, bringing his leg in front of you, over your shoulder. Sweep a little if you have to. (8-10) You now have the second opponent's leg with the same position as you originally started from. Your right and left hands still hang on to their ankles. Move your right hand out of the way, so that your left foot can get behind the second opponent's supporting leg. Bring your left hand in front of you and over your shoulder. At the same time, turn your body to the right. Keep your left leg strong at all times. That is the leg your opponent is being tripped by. (11) Get ready to strike both with your punch.

2

3

5

6

8

9

11

1

2

3

4

DEFENSE FOR SIDE KICK

(1&2) When your opponent starts kicking, it is common sense that the target will be the front part of your body. (3) By this time you should have figured out where the kick is aimed. (4) As his side kick reaches for your chest, move your body back without moving your stance, swaying so that your opponent cannot reach you at his full extension. At his full extension, put your right hand above his kicking foot and left hand below. At this point, there is no way he can kick you again, because he already reached his extension

5

6

and his power has been delivered. If he wants to kick again, he has to bring his knee back. Therefore, it is perfectly okay to get in close to his kick. (5) Grab his heel with your right hand as your left hand grabs the bottom of his instep. (6) Lower your right knee with most of your weight upon it. (7) Turn your hands clockwise. (8) When your opponent moves in the same direction in which you are twisting his leg, follow through as much as possible. He should then be forced to the ground.

7

8